Voices of CONSEQUENCES
ENRICHMENT SERIES

Unlocking the Prison Doors

(12 Points to Inner Healing and Restoration)

BY: JAMILA T. DAVIS
VOLUME 1

Curriculum Guide

Voices of Consequences Enrichment Series
Unlocking the Prison Doors: 12 Points to Inner Healing and Restoration
Curriculum Guide

Copyright © 2012 by Jamila T. Davis

All rights reserved. This book or any portion thereof may not be reproduced or used in any manner whatsoever without the express written permission of the publisher, except for the use of brief quotations in a book review.

This book is a nondenominational, faith-based, instruction manual. It was created to inspire, uplift and encourage incarcerated women to overcome the dilemmas that led to their imprisonment and to provide instructions to help them obtain emotional healing. The author shares the strategies she has utilized, both spiritual and non-spiritual, to gain emotional wholeness. This book is not written to promote any set of religious beliefs, although it does encourage readers to be open to receiving assistance from their "Higher Power" as they know Him.

The author of this book does not claim to have originated any techniques or principles shared in this book. She has simply formulated a system of proven strategies, from her research and experience during imprisonment, that her readers can utilize to obtain healing and restoration. A comprehensive list of references used to create this work is located in the back of this book. Readers are encouraged to use this reference list to obtain additional books to further their learning experience.

Printed in the United States of America
First Printing, 2012

Library of Congress Control Number: 2012941665
ISBN: 978-0-9855807-2-8

Voices International Publications
196-03 Linden Blvd.
St. Albans, NY 11412
"Changing Lives A Page At A Time."
www.vocseries.com

Typesetting and Design by: Jana Rade www.impactstudiosonline.com
Edited by: Ann Lockwood, Kat Masurak and Theresa Squillacote

TABLE OF CONTENTS

Introduction 1

Course Outline: Unlocking the Prison Doors Curriculum 3

Syllabus/Course Outline 5

Lesson Plan – Session #1/Learning to Surrender 9

Lesson Plan – Session #2/Learning to Surrender 11

Lesson Plan – Session #3/Accepting Help from Our "Higher Power" 13

Lesson Plan – Session #4/Accepting Help from Our "Higher Power" 15

Lesson Plan – Session #5/Getting to the Root of the Problem-
"Who Am I?" 19

Lesson Plan – Session #6/Getting to the Root of the Problem -
"Who Am I?" 23

Lesson Plan – Session #7/Acknowledging Our Shortcomings 27

Lesson Plan – Session #8/Acknowledging Our Shortcomings 29

Lesson Plan – Session #9/Accepting Responsibility for Our Actions 31

Lesson Plan – Session #10/Accepting Responsibility for Our Actions . . . 33

Lesson Plan – Session #11/Closing the Doors to Shame and Guilt 35

Lesson Plan – Session #12/Closing the Doors to Shame and Guilt 37

Lesson Plan – Session #13/Forgiving Others Who Have Wronged Us . . . 39

Lesson Plan – Session #14/Forgiving Others Who Have Wronged Us . . . 41

Lesson Plan – Session #15/Changing Our "Stinking Thinking" 43

Lesson Plan – Session #16/Changing Our "Stinking Thinking" 45

Lesson Plan – Session #17/Managing Your Emotions 47

Lesson Plan – Session #18/Managing Your Emotions 49

Lesson Plan – Session #19/Learning to Care for "Self" 51

Lesson Plan – Session #20/Learning to Care for "Self" 53

Lesson Plan – Session #21/Alternatives to Crime 55

Lesson Plan – Session #22/Alternatives to Crime 57

Lesson Plan – Session #23/Each Day Becoming a Better "Self" 59

Lesson Plan – Session #24/Each Day Becoming a Better "Self" 61

HANDOUT #1 – Introduction to Unlocking the Prison Doors 63

HANDOUT #2 – Learning to Surrender 65

HANDOUT #3 – Accepting Help from Our "Higher Power" 67

HANDOUT #4 – Getting to the Root of the Problem—"Who Am I?" 71

HANDOUT #5 – Getting to the Root of the Problem—"Who Am I?" 73

HANDOUT #6 – Getting to the Root of the Problem—"Who Am I?" 77

HANDOUT #7 – Acknowledging Our Shortcomings 85

HANDOUT #8 – Acknowledging Our Shortcomings 89

HANDOUT #9 – Accepting Responsibility for Our Actions 93

HANDOUT #10 – Accepting Responsibility for Our Actions 97

HANDOUT #11 – Closing the Doors to Shame and Guilt 99

HANDOUT #12 – Closing the Doors to Shame and Guilt 101

HANDOUT #13 – Forgiving Others Who Have Wronged Us 103

HANDOUT #14 – Changing Our "Stinking Thinking" 105

HANDOUT #15 – Managing Your Emotions 107

HANDOUT #16 – Learning to Care for "Self" 111

HANDOUT #17 – Learning to Care for "Self" 113

HANDOUT #18 – Alternatives to Crime. 117

FINAL EXAMINATION 121

INTRODUCTION

The Voices of Consequences Enrichment Series was created to help incarcerated women successfully rehabilitate and heal from past inner wounds. It is the goal of this series to empower women, enabling them to successfully transition back into society, by equipping them with the tools they will need to overcome obstacles—including the stigma of being an ex-convict.

This series is written from a unique standpoint. Unlike many other self-help books, this series is written by an inmate, Jamila T. Davis, for other inmates. Her real-life experiences of imprisonment have given her an insightful viewpoint of the lifestyles and criminal thinking patterns of convicted felons. As a result, inmates aren't spoken down to; they are addressed, face-to-face, with the truths of their current situation, in a way they can understand. These books will make them laugh, and at times cause them to cry. They provide the magnifying glass lenses needed for incarcerated women to take a closer, accurate assessment of their crimes, past behavioral patterns, and the effects their lives have had on themselves as well as others. At the same time these books will inspire and encourage readers to make a positive change, empowering them to become their very best!

The first book in this series, entitled *Unlocking the Prison Doors*, introduces readers to the need for restoration and emotional healing. It exposes readers to their character flaws and the negative effects these flaws have had on their lives. It also teaches readers how to identify their weaknesses and how to change them.

This Curriculum Guide was developed to assist proctors to administer group sessions where the curriculum of *Unlocking the Prison Doors* is taught.

This guide provides fundamental assistance on how each session should be administered, providing detailed lesson plans including suggestions, group activities and written assignments that can be utilized to illuminate the message taught in the text.

Group sessions will heighten the effects of the techniques taught in the text because they give readers the chance to share their experiences and learn from the experiences shared by others in their group. These sessions can be powerful because they lend participants the support of others who are also experiencing similar dilemmas in life, causing the healing process to be embraced and supported. Participants quickly recognize they are not alone in experiencing life's difficulties.

This guide is written based on the author's experience in group pilot sessions administered during her incarceration. She has skillfully organized exercises and discussion questions that will prompt positive responses from group participants. They are arranged for implementation in this guide.

For best results, utilize this Curriculum Guide along with the Text and Workbook/Journal. Follow each session and allow your group sessions to be open to expand on further discussions and questions brought up in your group.

It is essential to note that healing during these sessions is a process that can be very painful and expose shocking and disheartening events that led to imprisonment. Therefore, allow participants to be as comfortable as possible and encourage each of them to share their stories and input that relate to the subject matter, without going off course. When you come in contact with a participant who needs further assistance or has a question that you are not equipped to answer, please refer them to the prison's psychology department.

Groups should never exceed 20-25 people in each session. Smaller groups allow intimacy and privacy that would not be afforded in larger group settings.

The purpose of each group is to comprehend the message, share findings and heal. This manual is designed to assist proctors in obtaining these results.

The best proctors are those who have experienced similar life adversities as the participants, or those who understand and sympathize with the lifestyles of incarcerated women. Proctors need no special teaching skills.

As a proctor, you must be open-minded. Listen carefully to the stories and input of the women. Then, provide them with advice and suggestions based on the text. Effective results are obtained when the proctor lovingly guides the participants on the path to healing.

Congratulations on your new endeavor as a proctor! If you follow the guidance listed in this guide you will witness amazing results! Never forget that as a proctor you are empowered to change lives! Your comments and compassion can and will make a difference.

COURSE OUTLINE: UNLOCKING THE PRISON DOORS CURRICULUM

REQUIRED TEXT:

- Davis, Jamila. Voices of Consequences Enrichment Series: Unlocking the Prison Doors. Voices International Publications, New York: 2012
- Davis, Jamila. Voices of Consequences Enrichment Series: Unlocking the Prison Doors Workbook/Journal. Voices International Publications, New York: 2012

MATERIALS NEEDED:

1) Pen or a pencil.
2) Loose-leaf paper or a notebook for occasional in-class handwritten assignments.
3) Manila folder to store completed assignments and class handouts.

COURSE DESCRIPTION:

Unlocking the Prison Doors is a course designed to assist incarcerated women in identifying the need for restoration and emotional healing in their lives. This course exposes women to their own character flaws and negative choices that have had ill effects on their lives. Group participants learn techniques they can utilize to identify their own weaknesses and how to change them.

Activities will include reading selections from the Text and Workbook/Journal; participation through in-class discussion and essay response; reading and responding to peer examples (both orally and in writing); and completing questions and written assignments in the Workbook/Journal.

COURSE OBJECTIVE:

It is the goal of the *Unlocking the Prison Doors* course to empower women to heal by encouraging them to forgive themselves and others who have abused them in their past. Healing includes overcoming negative emotions such as anger, fear, worry, doubt, shame and guilt.

Participants will further be enlightened, through the VOC curriculum, to view their crimes from the standpoint of their victims, helping them to genuinely accept responsibility for their actions.

ATTENDANCE:

Group sessions will be held twice a week. Attending each class is mandatory, as each class builds on the previous lesson. Missing more than two group sessions may result in automatic withdrawal from the group.

Promptness is essential! Coming to class late by ten minutes or more, three times will constitute one absence (except for the first session).

REQUIREMENTS:

Each participant must commit to attending all classes, reading the text, completing written assignments and participating in group discussions.

Each participant is sworn to confidentiality. What is discussed in class <u>MUST</u> not be taken out of the group! Any participant caught discussing the personal business of others discussed amongst the group will be expelled and withdrawn from the group <u>immediately</u>!

DURATION:

12 weeks/24 sessions.

GROUP SIZE:

2-25 participants.

Syllabus/Course Outline

I. INTRODUCTION

- Understanding the VOC series
- Course objective
- Course description
- Requirements

II. LEARNING TO SURRENDER

- Developing an open mind
- Accepting life as unmanageable in current state
- Acquiring the willingness to change

III. ACCEPTING HELP FROM OUR "HIGHER POWER"

- Learning the importance of a "Higher Power"
- God's will versus our own will
- God's purpose for allowing life's obstacles
- Companionship throughout your journey: Developing a relationship with God

IV. GETTING TO THE ROOT OF THE PROBLEM—"WHO AM I?"

- The importance of self-discovery
- The masks of society
- Exposing our true "self"
- The enemy of our souls
- Examining how we became who we are
- Analyzing our true likes and dislikes
- Codependency

V. ACKNOWLEDGING OUR SHORTCOMINGS

- The detriments of denial
- Identifying past adverse behavior/areas of weakness
- Identifying past virtuous behavior/positive characteristics
- Pinpointing negative influences
- The importance of detachment

VI. ACCEPTING RESPONSIBILITY FOR OUR ACTIONS

- Understanding the importance of accepting responsibility
- Pinpointing our past wrongdoings
- Identifying our victims
- Evaluating the hardships we caused others
- Accepting the need to change our harmful behavior

VII. CLOSING THE DOORS TO SHAME AND GUILT

- Identifying shame and guilt
- Understanding the detriments of shame and guilt
- Learning how to deal with the past by accepting it, then letting it go!
- The purpose of remorse
- The importance of self-forgiveness

VIII. FORGIVING OTHERS WHO HAVE WRONGED US

- Dealing with the pain of our past
- Identifying those who have hurt us
- The importance of forgiveness
- The detriments of unforgiveness
- Learning how to forgive
- Developing the courage to forgive

IX. CHANGING OUR "STINKING THINKING"

- The power of our thoughts
- The law of attraction
- The detriments of "stinking thinking"
- The virtue of positive thinking
- The importance of how we view our circumstances
- Learning how to control/change our thinking

X. MANAGING OUR EMOTIONS

- Identifying our feelings and emotions and understanding their purpose
- Learning the detriments of anger
- Learning how to deal with anger
- Learning the detriments of fear, worry and doubt
- Learning how to overcome fear, worry and doubt

XI. LEARNING TO CARE FOR "SELF"

- Becoming in tune with "self"
- Developing self-pride and self-esteem
- Discovering how to tap into our inner joy
- Evaluating what makes us happy
- Evaluating what makes us sad
- Learning how to protect "self"
- Learning how to reward "self"

XII. ALTERNATIVES TO CRIME

- Learning the need to become responsible and mature
- Pinpointing the consequences of crime
- Assessing our skill sets and talents
- Resources for ex-felons
- Developing trades and skill sets
- Occupations/Training

XIII. EACH DAY BECOMING A BETTER "SELF"

- Learning how to perform continuous self-assessment throughout the day
- Reviewing techniques and strategies for self-improvement
- The importance of visualization—seeing yourself as being successful
- Monitoring our thoughts daily
- Developing a plan for self-improvement

Lesson Plan – Session #1/Learning to Surrender

GOAL: Introduce participants to the VOC Series, course objectives and the rules/requirements of the group. Prepare students to be open-minded to the need for change.

- Introduce participants to the *Voices of Consequences Enrichment Series* by:
    - Discussing and reviewing Course Description, Course Objectives Requirements and Materials needed (located under Course Outline on pages 3-4).
- Have participants take turns reading aloud the Introduction to Unlocking the Prison Doors in the text, pages 1-8.
- Based on the Introduction reading, have the participants complete Handout #1, located in the back of this book.
  Questions in this Handout include:
    1) What do you think you can learn from this course?
    2) How does this course differ from typical group sessions?
    3) Are you willing to be open-minded as you embark on this new journey's "Mission Change?"
    4) What supplies will you need during this course?
    5) What requirements will you need to fulfill in order to complete this course?
- After group discussion, have participants take turns reading aloud Chapter 1: Learning to Surrender in the text, on pages 9-16.
- Open discussion: what are the participants' thoughts and feelings about this chapter.
- Have participants complete Handout # 2, based on the poem "I Surrender- a Prisoner's Cry, in the text on pages 10-13.

Questions in this Handout include:
1) What similarities do you have to the women's lives mentioned in the poem?
2) What events in life led these women astray? Can you relate? Why or why not?
3) What poor choices did these women make? Why were these choices poor?
4) What does the poet suggest women do if they want to change?
5) Are you ready to surrender and open your life up to change? Why or why not?

- Have participants take turns answering the questions in Handout #2. Allow each question to be open for discussion.
- Close your group session with the affirmation of surrender located in the last paragraph on page 15 in the text (have the participants say this affirmation out loud together):

   "I admit that my life has become unmanageable. I recognize that I'm at a point in my life where I need to experience change. I realize that I cannot make it by myself. I formally surrender."
- Congratulate participants for their courage and give instructions on the Homework Assignment.

HOMEWORK ASSIGNMENT

Have the group read Chapter 1 in the Workbook/Journal and answer the questions in Chapter 1, and start Writing Assignment-Journal Entry #1.

Lesson Plan – Session #2/Learning to Surrender

GOAL: **Have participants become aware of the poor choices they have made in their past that led to incarceration. Through the process of self-evaluation, help participants develop a willingness to surrender.**

- Start your group session by having participants read aloud the affirmation of surrender on page 15, in the text:
    > "I admit that my life has become unmanageable. I recognize that I'm at a point in my life where I need to experience change. I realize that I cannot make it by myself. I formally surrender."
- Have participants read Chapter 1/Review in the Workbook/Journal on page 5.
- After reading Chapter 1/Review in the Workbook, have participants take turns answering questions 1-10, on pages 6-8. Allow these questions to become group discussions by giving more than one person an opportunity to answer each question.
- After group discussion, have participants read aloud the Example section of Chapter 1, on page 9, in the Workbook/Journal. Then, have participants take turns answering questions #1-5, on pages 10-11, in the Workbook/Journal. Again, allow multiple participants to share their answers and feelings about the example in a group discussion.
- Based on the group discussions have the participants review their Writing Assignment-Journal Entry #1, which they started for homework, and give them an opportunity to complete their assignment based on their new discoveries.
- Ask for volunteers to share their journal entries. Let each journal entry be open for group discussion.
  *Note: Never force anyone to share their writings. Let each participant open up when they feel comfortable doing so.

- Congratulate your group for their participation and courage and give out the Homework Assignment.

HOMEWORK ASSIGNMENT

Have the group read Chapter 2: Accepting Help from Our "Higher Power," in the text.

Lesson Plan – Session #3/Accepting Help from Our "Higher Power"

GOAL: Have participants discover the importance of having the assistance of their "Higher Power" throughout this journey. Help participants understand God's purpose for allowing life's obstacles.

- Have participants take turns reading Chapter 2: Accepting Help from Our "Higher Power," in the text pages 17-25.
- Based on the reading, ask the group to complete questions #1-3 on Handout #3, which includes the following questions, to be open for discussion:
    1) Has this chapter changed your perception about God or the need for a "Higher Power?" Why or why not?
    2) Based on this reading, has your perception of your current situation changed? Why or why not?
    3) Do you believe God allowed your current circumstances of imprisonment for a greater purpose? If so, explain.
- Have participants review the example in the text about Tracy, beginning on page 22, ending on page 24.
- Based on the example, have participants answer questions #4-6 on Handout #3, which includes the following questions, to be open for group discussion:
    - Can you relate to Tracy or have you seen others in prison experience the same hardships as Tracy had with her husband?
    - What did God allow Tracy's hardships to reveal to her?
    - Why do you think Sam changed when Tracy became incarcerated? Did he ever really love her? Why or why not?
    - What good came out of Tracy's incarceration?

- How did Tracy benefit from developing a relationship with her "Higher Power?"
- Close your group by asking the participants if they are willing to allow God into their lives to help them through this journey.
- If they agree, with no pressure, ask them to jointly repeat the prayer on page 25 pages 24-25 in the text together:

    "God, today I invite You into my life. I desire to know You better. I admit I am powerless over my current situation and circumstances. I recognize I am in a stage of my life that requires change. I realize that I can do nothing by my own strength. I need a Power greater than myself to restore me. I now turn over all my problems and burdens to You. I ask You for the strength I need to travel through this journey. I surrender my will and my expected outcome, and I turn over the results to You. Come into my life today. Restore my heart, mind and soul. Show me the way You intend for me to go and provide me with the necessary help and resources to get there. Amen."

- Congratulate the group on their success and provide the Homework Assignment.

HOMEWORK ASSIGNMENT

Have the group read Chapter 2, in the Workbook/ Journal, and answer the questions in Chapter 2. Additionally, have participants start Writing Assignment-Journal Entry #2.

Lesson Plan – Session #4/Accepting Help from Our "Higher Power"

GOAL: Introduce participants to the difference of God's will versus our own will and the purpose of obstacles.
Enlighten participants on how they can develop a relationship with their "Higher Power."

- Start your group session by having participants read aloud the prayer on pages 24-25 in the text together:

    "God, today I invite you into my life. I desire to know You better. I admit I am powerless over my current situation and circumstances. I recognize I am in a stage of my life that requires change. I realize that I can do nothing by my own strength. I need a Power greater than myself to restore me. I now turn over all my problems and burdens to You. I ask You for the strength I need to travel through this journey. I surrender my will and my expected outcome, and I turn over the results to You. Come into my life today. Restore my heart, mind and soul. Show me the way You intend for me to go and provide me with the necessary help and resources to get there. Amen."

- After reading the affirmation of spiritual commitment, ask the group the following questions, open for group discussion:
    1) What does this commitment really entail?
    2) Why is a serious commitment needed during this journey?
    3) What does this commitment personally mean to you? Will it change the way you normally think and act? Why or why not?
- Have participants take turns reading Chapter 2/Review in the Workbook/Journal on pages 13-14.
- After reading Chapter 2/Review in the Workbook/Journal, have participants take turns answering questions 1-10, on pages 14-16.

Allow these questions to become group discussions by giving more than one person an opportunity to answer each question.

*Note: During discussion time explain how God's will often differs from our own, but He knows what is best for us. Elaborate in discussions that show how God uses obstacles to bring us into His will.

- After the group discussion, have participants read aloud the Example Section of Chapter 2, on pages 16-18, in the Workbook/Journal. Then, have participants take turns answering questions #1-5, on pages 18-19, in the Workbook/Journal. Again, allow multiple participants to share their answers and feelings about the example in a group discussion.
- After the group discussion, ask the group the following questions, open for discussion:
    1) How do you normally communicate with God?
    2) Do you believe He hears and answers your prayers? Why or why not?
    3) Are you specific when you pray?
    4) Do you feel that you bother God when you pray about small things?

*Note: During discussion time explain and emphasize that we can go to God with any of our problems whether large or small. God is never bothered. He is actually honored that we choose to come to Him and rely on Him, rather than others. During this journey make it a habit to bring all of your experiences, both good and bad. One way to accomplish this goal is by writing to Him.

- Have participants complete Journal Entry #2-Writing Assignment, on page 19, in the Workbook/Journal.

*Note: Emphasize the importance of being honest and specific in their letters to God. Also, advise participants that they should make their letter writing a daily habit to track their progress and answers to prayer.

- Ask for volunteers to share their journal entries. Let each journal entry be open for group discussion.

*Note: Some participants may not be comfortable sharing their letters to God. Others may wish to share their letters. Both are alright. The letters can give others ideas on how to present their requests to God and what to ask.

- Remind the participants of the importance of developing a relationship with God and accepting His will to successfully complete this journey. Congratulate them on their progress and provide their Homework Assignment.

HOMEWORK ASSIGNMENT:

Have the group read Chapter 3: Getting to the Root of the Problem - Who Am I?, in the text.

Lesson Plan – Session #5/Getting to the Root of the Problem–"Who Am I?"

GOAL: Introduce participants to the importance of self-discovery and the beauty of "self," preparing participants to gain the courage to peel back the masks that represent their false "self."

- Have participants take turns reading, in the text, Chapter 3: Getting to the Root of the Problem - "Who Am I?" Read pages 27-33. Stop for discussion after reading paragraph 2 on page 33.
- Have participants complete Handout #4. Questions on this Handout include:
    1) Did you receive the love, care, and the compassion you needed as a child?
    2) Did you feel safe and secure as a child? Why or why not?
    3) Were you ever violated sexually or physically? Explain.
    4) Did you ever experience verbal abuse? Explain.
    5) Were both of your parents there to raise you? Explain.
    6) Did your life turn out to be similar to those whom you were around growing up? Explain.
- After the participants answer the questions, ask for volunteers to describe their childhood experiences and how they feel these experiences influenced their lives. Compare the effects of childhood experiences in open discussion.
  *Note: Don't force anyone to share their experiences. Let each person open up as much as they feel comfortable doing.
- After the group discussion continue reading Chapter 3 in the text, from page 33 to page 36.
- After reading the first paragraph on page 36, stop and have participants review the questions asked, which are complied in

Handout #5. Have participants complete Handout #5. Allow these questions to be open for discussion.

1) How do you currently feel about yourself? Why?
2) What can you do to improve yourself?
3) How difficult will this be to accomplish?
4) How do you treat others?
5) Would you like others to treat you that way?
6) How strong are the relationships you have developed with others?
7) Are these relationships positive? Why or why not?
8) What do you like to do in your spare time?
9) Are these activities productive? Why or why not?
10) What other productive activities do you think you should start to participate in?
11) What are your goals in life?
12) What steps will it take to achieve these goals?
13) What is the greatest achievement you have obtained in your life?
14) How did you feel when you accomplished this achievement?
15) What other great achievements will you strive for in the future?

*Note: Allow your group adequate time to write down the answers to the questions. Explain to them that these questions are what they will use to analyze and to realize who they truly are and what they want to become. Let them know it is okay not to have the answers to all these questions, but that by the time they complete this series they will have answers for each of them. There is no need to review these answers in class. They are simply a part of self-discovery.

- After the participants have completed their written answers, have them continue taking turns reading pages 36-44, in the text.
- After the chapter reading, ask participants to share what they have learned about themselves from the group session, and what they need to work on. Turn these answers into a group discussion.
- End the session by having all the participants read aloud, together, the prayer on page 43, in the text:

> *"God, I thank You for coming into my life and revealing to me some of the roots of my problems. I ask that You daily reveal to me my shortcomings and grant me the strength and ability to correct them. Help me to become aware of 'self' and guide me through this process of healing. Give me insight into my problems and provide me with divine solutions. Cleanse my heart and mind of all defilement and prepare me for this journey. Empower me to remain honest and open throughout this process. Help me to completely heal and allow me to be made whole. Amen."*

- Congratulate the group on their success and provide the Homework Assignment.

HOMEWORK ASSIGNMENT

Have the group read Chapter 3, in the Workbook/ Journal, and answer the questions in Chapter 3. Additionally, have participants start Writing Assignment - Journal Entry #3.

Also, distribute Handout #6, located in the back of this book. Encourage students to complete the handout to be ready for discussion during the next group session.

Lesson Plan – Session #6/Getting to the Root of the Problem - "Who Am I?"

GOAL: Have participants discover their true "self" by uncovering the root of their problems that led them astray.
Help participants develop the courage to be themselves, and to be by themselves, when necessary, by revealing to them the detriments of codependency.

- Start your group session by having participants read aloud, together, the prayer on page 43, in the text:

    "God, I thank You for coming into my life and revealing to me some of the roots of my problems. I ask that You daily reveal to me my shortcomings and grant me the strength and ability to correct them. Help me to become aware of 'self' and guide me through this process of healing. Give me insight into my problems and provide me with divine solutions. Cleanse my heart and mind of all defilement and prepare me for this journey. Empower me to remain honest and open throughout this process. Help me to completely heal and allow me to be made whole. Amen."

- Ask participants if they have any new findings about themselves or anything they need to work on after reading Chapter 3 and completing the homework assignment. Open this question for group discussion.
- After the discussion, have participants take turns reading Chapter 3/Review, in the Workbook/Journal on pages 21-24.
    After reading Chapter 3/Review, in the Workbook/Journal, have participants take turns answering questions 1-10, on pages 24-26. Allow these questions to be turned into group discussions by giving more than one person an opportunity to answer each question.

Note: Encourage participants to give examples and elaborate on their answers. Through this discussion participants should be revealing the root of their problems and discovering who they truly are.

- After the group discussion, have participants read aloud the Example section of Chapter 3, on pages 26-28, in the Workbook/Journal. Then, have participants take turns answering questions 1-5, on pages 28-29, in the Workbook/Journal. Again, allow multiple participants to share their answers and feelings about the example in a group discussion.
- Have participants complete Journal Entry #3-Writing Assignment, on page 29, in the Workbook/Journal.
- Ask for volunteers to share their enlightenment regarding childhood influences on their behavior by providing examples through their life experiences. (Ex: What experiences in your childhood led you to go astray? Did you feel that childhood trauma or abuse was your fault?)

Note: This topic may be very sensitive and emotional. Make sure the environment is as comfortable as possible for them to be open and share. Be ready to lend encouragement and support. Again, never force anyone to share! Let everyone participate as they feel comfortable.

- After this discussion, have participants review pages 37-41 in the text, on codependency. After participants review the text, ask them to complete Handout #6, located in the back of this book, which they were handed out for Homework. These questions on codependency, included in Handout #6, are listed below:
    1) Describe codependency in your own words.
    2) Why do people become codependent on others?
    3) Is codependency healthy? Why or why not?
    4) Give an example of codependent behavior in prison.
    5) Why do codependent people falsely believe they are in control or have power over another person?
    6) Can we control people? Why or why not?
    7) What is the solution to codependency?
    8) How do we develop healthy boundaries in relationships?
    9) What is "disabling" a person?
    10) What is "enabling" a person?

- After participants have completed Handout #6, allow them to take turns answering each question. Open the questions for discussion. Note: Allow the discussion to elaborate on codependency and its detriments. Encourage examples that show the effects of codependency.
- Close the session by asking the group, recapping what the participants discovered in the group about who they are, how did they become who they are? And, what have they discovered that they could do to change their lives?
- Congratulate the participants on their progress and provide their Homework Assignment.

HOMEWORK ASSIGNMENT

Have the group read Chapter 4: Acknowledging Our Shortcomings, in the text.

Lesson Plan – Session #7/Acknowledging Our Shortcomings

GOAL: Prepare participants to dethrone denial and to honestly evaluate their past adverse and beneficial character traits, by educating them to the detriments of denial.

- This session will require the complete honesty of your group. Therefore, prepare your group to do some soul searching and expose their shortcomings. Warn them that this process is not easy, yet it is necessary to properly heal and rehabilitate.
- Have participants take turns reading Chapter 4: Acknowledging Our Shortcomings, pages 45-50 in the text. Stop reading after the third paragraph on page 50.
- Then, have participants fill out the Moral Inventory List of Weaknesses, on pages 33-41, in the Workbook/ Journal.
- When the participants complete this list, go over the questions, and ask who answered yes to each question. Then, invite them to elaborate on their behavior. Ask: why do they behave this way, and do they think it is right or wrong?
- Have participants take turns reading in the text pages 50-51. Stop reading after the third paragraph on page 51.
- Then, have participants fill out the Moral Inventory of Good Character Traits on pages 41-45, in the Workbook/Journal.
- When the participants complete this list, review the questions, and ask who answered yes to each question. Then, invite them to elaborate on their behavior. Ask: why do they behave this way, and do they think it is right or wrong?
- Based on their self-analysis, have participants complete Handout #7, located in the back of this book. The handout is a self-analysis that asks the following questions:

1) Who am I? (List both the positive and negative characteristics that you discovered through the Moral Inventory of Weaknesses and Good Character Traits. Utilize the evaluation grids in the Workbook/Journal on page 40 and page 45.)
2) Who do I want to be? (Think about the areas you want to improve in and write out the characteristics you desire to have.)

- Encourage participants to share their answers with the group.
- Then, explain to the participants that they have embarked on the healing process. Healing is continuous self-discovery. Be open to identify your faults, so you can overcome them.
- Close the session having participants read, together, the prayer on page 55, in the text.

    "God, I thank You for the strength to expose my shortcomings. I understand that if I am unable to recognize my faults, I will also be unable to fix them. Help me to see myself through Your eyes. Daily show me the characteristics You wish me to change. Let me know when I fall short of Your standards. Gently nudge me and guide me back into the correct direction. I now ask for the strength I need to travel through this journey of restoration. Heal me and make me whole. Amen."

- Congratulate the participants on their progress and provide their Homework Assignment.

HOMEWORK ASSIGNMENT

Instruct participants to read Chapter 4/Review in the Workbook/Journal and answer the questions on page 44. Also, encourage participants to start Journal Entry #4: Writing Assignment on page 52, in the Workbook/Journal.

Lesson Plan – Session #8/Acknowledging Our Shortcomings

GOAL: Enlighten participants to the danger of bad associations and negative influences, and the importance of detachment from these relationships.
Have participants perform a self-analysis of bad relationships, so they can prepare to detach from them.

- Start your group session by asking participants to read aloud, together, the prayer on page 55, in the text.
    > *"God, I thank You for the strength to expose my shortcomings. I understand that if I am unable to recognize my faults, I will also be unable to fix them. Help me to see myself through Your eyes. Daily show me the characteristics You wish me to change. Let me know when I fall short of Your standards. Gently nudge me and guide me back into the correct direction. I now ask for the strength I need to travel through this journey of restoration. Heal me and make me whole. Amen."*
- Ask the group to begin by sharing any new discoveries the participants have made. Also, ask if they feel these sessions have helped them on their journey to healing and restoration. If so, how?
- After the discussion, have participants read page 51, in the text, (staring at the fourth paragraph) to page 52 (finish at the end of the third paragraph).
- Have participants complete the Bad Relationships Inventory, in the Workbook/Journal on pages 46-50.
- Go over answers with the group, and ask if they have found any common denominators, or negative influences.
- Have participants read page 52, in the text,(starting at the fourth paragraph) to page 55 (finish at the end of the third paragraph).

Then, have participants complete Handout #8 (located in the back of this book) on Negative Relationships.
- Then, instruct them to complete the answers to the questions on the Handout in a group discussion session.
- Have participants take turns, reading aloud, Chapter 4/Review, in the Workbook/Journal, on pages 31-33.
- Then, ask participants to answer questions 1-5 on pages 50-51, in the Workbook/Journal.
- Allow participants to take turns answering questions in an open discussion forum.
- Have participants complete Journal Entry #4: Writing Assignment on page 52, in the Workbook/Journal.
- Invite participants to volunteer and share their journal entries.
- Congratulate participants on their growth and discoveries, and provide the Homework Assignment.

HOMEWORK ASSIGNMENT

Have participants read Chapter 5: Accepting Responsibility for Our Actions, in the text.

Lesson Plan – Session #9/Accepting Responsibility for Our Actions

GOAL: Enlighten participants on the importance of accepting responsibility for past wrongdoings, and prepare participants to be willing and able to accept responsibility. Identify the adverse actions that led to imprisonment, and identify the role played and the consequences endured as a result.

- Start the group by asking the following questions, to be open for discussion.
    1) Describe in your own words what is accepting responsibility for our actions.
    2) Why are many people trapped in denial, unable to take responsibility for their own shortcomings?
    3) Even if someone else influenced your actions or influenced you to be involved in something you would not ordinarily be a part of, why are you still held responsible?
- After the group discussion, have participants take turns reading Chapter 5: Accepting Responsibility for Our Actions, in the text, on pages 57-70.
- For open discussion, ask: what are the participants' thoughts and feelings about this chapter?
- Have participants complete Handout #9, located in the back of this book. The questions on the handout include the following:
    1) After reading Chapter 5 in the text, describe in your own words what adverse actions you took led to your imprisonment.
    2) What role did you play in these actions?
    3) What are the consequences you have had to endure because of your behavior?

4) Do you regret your decision to take part in this behavior? Why or why not?
5) Do you fully accept responsibility for your wrongdoings? Explain.

- After participants complete the Handout, encourage the group to share each of their answers.

    Note: Acceptance of responsibility for adverse behavior is a vital prerequisite in order for each participant to heal and regain footing on the right track in life. Therefore, allow this discussion to be in-depth, and allow other participants to comment on the answers of group participants.

- Close this session by asking participants to do further soul-searching and to think about the victims that have suffered because of their past adverse actions. Then, have participants read the prayer, aloud, together, on pages 68-69, in the text:

    "God, today I realize the effects of my crime on others. Today I am truly remorseful. I admit I was wrong, and I ask that You please forgive me. Send Your divine healing to each one of my victims. Provide them with the love and support they need each day. Help them to also forgive me, and let them see how truly remorseful I am. I ask You for another chance to make the correct decisions in life. Rekindle the bonds and ties of my family members and loved ones. Open their hearts to also forgive me. Today I stand before you as a new person. I promise to never make the same mistake of participating in any illegal activities. I now ask that You show me Your plan for my life, and lead and guide me in the way that I should go. Amen."

- Congratulate participants on their progress and provide the Homework Assignment.

HOMEWORK ASSIGNMENT

Have participants read Chapter 5/Review, in the Workbook/Journal, on pages 55-56, and answer questions #1-4 on pages 56-57. Also, have participants start Journal Entry #5-Writing Assignment.

Lesson Plan – Session #10/Accepting Responsibility for Our Actions

GOAL: Prepare participants to see their crimes from their victim's perspective. Then, help participants identify the victims who have suffered because of their adverse behavior, and the hardships that these victims have endured.

- Start the group by having participants read aloud, together, the prayer on pages 68-69, in the text:

    "God, today I realize the effects of my crime on others. Today I am truly remorseful. I admit I was wrong, and I ask that You please forgive me. Send Your divine healing to each one of my victims. Provide them with the love and support they need each day. Help them to also forgive me, and let them see how truly remorseful I am. I ask You for another chance to make the correct decisions in life. Rekindle the bonds and ties of my family members and loved ones. Open their hearts to forgive me. Today I stand before You as a new person. I promise to never make the same mistake of participating in any illegal activities. I now ask that You show me Your plan for my life, and lead and guide me in the way that I should go. Amen."

- Open your session by asking the following questions, to be open for group discussion:
    1) Have your thoughts changed about how your crime has affected others?
    2) Have you identified any additional victims, whom you had not considered as victims, that have suffered because of your actions?
    3) How have the readings and homework changed your point of view?

- Have the group briefly reread, quietly, the examples in the text, on pages 58-68.
- Then, have participants take turns reading aloud Chapter 5/Review, in the Workbook/Journal, on pages 55-56.
- Have participants take turns answering questions 1-12, on pages 56-60, in the Workbook/Journal. Allow more than one participant to share their answers and open questions for discussion.
- Allow the group to discuss, in detail, the three examples in Chapter 3. Ask participants the following questions, to be open for discussion:
    1) What key events caused the women in the examples to recognize how their actions truly affected their victims?
    2) Was this awakening necessary? Why or why not?
    3) What can we do to experience this same awakening concerning our crimes?
- Have participants complete Handout #10, located in the back of this book. The questions in the handout include the following:
    1) Identify the victims who have had to suffer because of your crime.
    2) In what ways have each of these victims suffered?
- Then, have participants complete the Journal Entry #5 - Writing Assignment on page 61, in the Workbook/ Journal.
- Ask for volunteers to share their journal entries with the group. Allow participants to give feedback and discuss each journal entry shared.
- Congratulate the group for their courage and progress, and provide their homework assignment.

HOMEWORK ASSIGNMENT

Have participants read Chapter 6: Closing the Doors to Shame and Guilt, in the text.

Lesson Plan – Session #11/Closing the Doors to Shame and Guilt

GOAL: Have participants understand and identify shame and guilt and the resulting detriments.
Prepare participants to examine the past and accept it. Then, let it go.

- Start the group session by asking participants the following questions, to be open for discussion:
    1) What new discoveries have you made about yourself since participating in the VOC program?
    2) Have you utilized any of the techniques or advice that you have learned through these group sessions?
    3) What areas, if any, do you believe you need to improve on in your life?
- Have participants take turns reading aloud Chapter 6: Closing the Doors to Shame and Guilt on pages 71-83, in the text.
- Open discussion on the participants' thoughts and feelings about this chapter.
- After the chapter reading, have participants complete Handout #11, located in the back of this book, which includes the following questions:
    1) Describe shame in your own words.
    2) Describe guilt in your own words.
    3) Take time to analyze your life. Are you currently holding on to any shame or guilt? Explain.
    4) Why is it important to rid yourself of shame and guilt?
    5) How can you begin to heal and become emotionally healthy?
- Have participants take turns answering the questions on the handout then open the topic for discussion.

Note: It is important that each participant understand what shame and guilt are and how they have been affected by these feelings. Therefore, allow your discussion to dig deep, and pinpoint areas of shame and guilt that the participants need to acknowledge and overcome.

- Ask all participants what negative effects the emotions shame and guilt have had in their lives now that they are able to analyze these feelings. Also, what ways or methods did they use to suppress guilt and shame? Open these questions for discussion.
- Close your session by having participants read aloud, together, the prayer in the text, on on page 82.
"God, I thank You for exposing my feelings of guilt and shame. I have dealt with them and today I released them. I did what at times seemed impossible to do: I forgave myself. Therefore, I am no longer bound to my past. Today I ask that You give me the strength to keep all guilt and shame from creeping back into my life. I ask that You lead positive people into my life, and rid me of those who would try to hinder me or constantly have me relive my past. Please give me the strength I need to sustain my freedom. Amen."
- Encourage participants to dig deeper and pull up any layers of shame and guilt they may have hidden inside. Congratulate them on their progress, and provide the Homework Assignment.

HOMEWORK ASSIGNMENT

Have participants read Chapter 6/Review, in the Workbook/Journal, on pages 63-65. Then, answer questions 1-10, on pages 66-68. Also, have participants start Journal Entry #6-Writing Assignment.

Lesson Plan – Session #12/Closing the Doors to Shame and Guilt

GOAL: Teach participants how to properly heal by learning from their mistakes and releasing the past.
Enlighten participants on the purpose of remorse and to the importance of self-forgiveness.

- Start the group by having participants read aloud, together, the prayer on page 82, in the text:

    "God, I thank You for exposing my feelings of guilt and shame. I have dealt with them and today I released them. I did what at times seemed impossible to do: I forgave myself. Therefore, I am no longer bound by my past. Today I ask that You give me the strength to keep all guilt and shame from creeping back into my life. I ask that You lead positive people into my life, and rid me of those who would try to hinder me or constantly have me relive my past. Please give me the strength I need to sustain my freedom. Amen."

- Have participants take turns reading aloud Chapter 6/Review on pages 63-65, in the Workbook/Journal.
- Ask participants to take turns answering questions 1-10 on pages 66-68. Let these questions be open for discussion.
- Have participants read the Example section, in the Workbook/Journal on pages 68-70.
- Then, have participants take turns answering questions 1-5 on pages pages 70-71. Allow these questions to be turned into an open discussion.
- Have participants complete Handout #12 in the back of this book. Then, allow participants to share their answers in a group discussion. The questions on this handout include:

1) Can you change the past? Why or why not?
2) Does your past dictate your future? Why or why not?
3) If you hate yourself, how will others treat you? Explain.
4) How can you take possession of your future?
5) What good do you hold inside that can be shared that would please your "Higher Power?"

- Have participants complete Journal Entry #6-Writing Assignment, in the Workbook/Journal on page 72.
- Ask for volunteers to share their journal entries with the group, to be open for discussion.
- Congratulate your group for their courage and progress, and provide their Homework Assignment.

HOMEWORK ASSIGNMENT

Read Chapter 7: Forgiving Others Who Have Wronged Us, in the text.

Lesson Plan – Session #13/Forgiving Others Who Have Wronged Us

**GOAL: Help participants identify inflictions and hardships that they have suffered in their past, enlightening them to those who have caused them pain.
Prepare participants to forgive those who have hurt them.**

- Have participants take turns, reading aloud, Chapter 7: Forgiving Others Who Have Wronged Us, in the text on pages 85-95.
- Open discussion by asking, what are the participants' thoughts and feeling about this chapter?
- Have participants complete Handout #13, located in the back of this book. Questions in the handout include:
    1) Write down the most significant events in your life that have caused you the most pain. (Summarize these events in a few sentences.)
    2) Write down the names of the individuals who hurt you as a result of these events.
    3) Have you forgiven the individuals who hurt you? Why or why not?
- Have participants complete the Abusers Chart on page 82, in the Workbook/Journal.
- Then, have participants review their answers to the Handout questions and the Abuser Chart in an open discussion.
  Note: This discussion will be emotional and painful. For the first time many participants will dig up painful emotions from their past. Therefore, be supportive and allow participants to share as they feel comfortable.
- Have participants answer the following questions in a group discussion:

1) Why is it important to forgive?
2) Why do many people fail to forgive others?
3) Are you willing to forgive those who hurt you in order to move ahead in life?

- Close your group session with the prayer on page 93, in the text:

   "God, You know all that I have experienced. You know every offense and abuse that has been committed against me. I ask that You give me the strength to forgive all those who have trespassed against me. I turn all of these abusive events and my abusers over to You now. I ask that You heal me of all the defilement that has been left in my life because of these offenses. Please deliver me from the hurt and pain I feel because of these events. I pray that You open the eyes of all those who have abused, mistreated, and betrayed me. Allow them to recognize that they have been used by the enemy. Touch their hearts and lead them onto the road of restoration. Help me to change my perception of the events and circumstances that have hindered me from achieving Your purpose for my life. Help me to recognize the good You have intended to come out of every obstacle, even in the midst of my turmoil. Please forgive me for any feelings of anger, resentment, bitterness, and unforgiveness towards You and anyone else for whom I may have harbored these feelings. I now understand You have a plan and a reason greater than I could ever imagine. I know the plans You have for me lead to the road of restoration. Please lead and guide me into this path. Keep me covered and protected from the schemes of the enemy. Shower me with Your love, affection, and favor all the days of my life. Most importantly, give me a heart that always forgives. Amen."

- Congratulate participants on their progress, and provide the Homework Assignment.

HOMEWORK ASSIGNMENT

Have participants read Chapter 7/Review in the Workbook/Journal, on pages 75-76. Then, answer questions 1-10, on pages 77-79. Also, have participants start Journal Entry #7 - Writing Assignment.

Lesson Plan – Session #14/Forgiving Others Who Have Wronged Us

---

GOAL: **Enlighten participants on the importance of forgiveness and the detriments of unforgiveness.**
Teach participants how to develop the courage to forgive and how to properly forgive others who have hurt them.

- Start the group by having participants read aloud, together, the prayer on page 93, in the text:

    "God, You know all that I have experienced. You know every offense and abuse that has been committed against me. I ask that You give me the strength to forgive all those who have trespassed against me. I turn all of these abusive events and my abusers over to You now. I ask that You heal me of all the defilement that has been left in my life because of these offenses. Please deliver me from the hurt and pain I feel because of these events. I pray that You open the eyes of all those who have abused, mistreated, and betrayed me. Allow them to recognize that they have been used by the enemy. Touch their hearts and lead them onto the road of restoration. Help me to change my perception of the events and circumstances that have hindered me from achieving Your purpose for my life. Help me to recognize the good You have intended to come out of every obstacle, even in the midst of my turmoil. Please forgive me for any feelings of anger, resentment, bitterness, and unforgiveness towards You and anyone else for whom I may have harbored these feelings. I now understand You have a plan and a reason greater than I could ever imagine. I know the plans You have for me lead to the road of restoration. Please lead and guide me into this path. Keep me covered and

> *protected from the schemes of the enemy. Shower me with Your love, affection, and favor all the days of my life. Most importantly, give me a heart that always forgives. Amen."*

- Have participants take turns reading aloud Chapter 7/Review in the Workbook/Journal on pages 75-76.
- Then, have participants answer questions 1-10 on pages 77-79 in the Workbook/Journal. Let each question be open for discussion.
- Have participants read the Example section of Chapter 7, in the Workbook/Journal on pages 79-80.
- Then, have participants answer questions 1-5 on pages 80-81, in the Workbook/Journal. Let each question be open for discussion.
- Have participants complete Journal Entry #7 - Writing Assignment, in the Workbook/Journal on page 84.
- Ask for volunteers to share their journal entries. Allow each journal entry to be open for discussion.
- Close your session by having participants read aloud, together, the affirmation on page 94, in the text, on the second paragraph (pause and allow the participants to say out loud each name of their abusers as instructed in the affirmation):

   > *"Today (list the names of your abusers), I am no longer emotionally bound to you. What you have done to me will no longer affect me. I realize today you are also a victim that has been used by the enemy. I have decided that I will no longer allow myself to have feelings of bitterness, anger, hate, or resentment towards you. I exercise my right to love you. I will love you by praying that God will open your eyes and allow you to see the pain you have caused me and others. My prayer is that you will one day change. In the meantime, I detach myself from you emotionally by forgiving you. Today I am free!"*

- Congratulate your group on their success, and provide the Homework Assignment.

HOMEWORK ASSIGNMENT

Have participants read Chapter 8: Changing Our "Stinking Thinking," in the text.

Lesson Plan – Session #15/Changing Our "Stinking Thinking"

GOAL: Teach participants the importance of their thoughts and the power of positive thinking.
Enlighten participants to the detriments of "stinking thinking."

- Start the group session by asking participants the following questions, to be open for discussion:
    1) How do you feel, so far, about the Voices of Consequences Enrichment Series?
    2) What have you learned that you believe will help improve your life?
    3) Have you identified any new areas that need improvement?
- Have participants take turns reading aloud Chapter 8: Changing our "Stinking Thinking," in the text on pages 97-109.
- Open discussion: what are the participants' thoughts and feelings about this Chapter?
- Have participants complete Handout #14, located in the back of this book. The questions in the handout include:
    1) Describe in your own words the definition of "stinking thinking."
    2) Do you believe "stinking thinking" led you to prison? Why or why not?
    3) What can you do to rid yourself of "stinking thinking?"
    4) Give an example of positive thinking that you can use in your life.
    5) Do your thoughts determine your future? Why or why not?
- Have participants take turns answering the questions on Handout #10. Allow each question to be open for discussion.

- Close your session by having participants read aloud, together, the prayer on page 108, in the text:
  > *"God, You are great, kind and merciful. Thank You for exposing me to the truth of the importance of my thinking. Today I desire to change my thoughts that have adversely affected my mind. Help me to fill my mind with positive thoughts. Send positive people into my life who can support and encourage me. Alert me when my thoughts are off track, and help me to quickly change them. I thank You now for a new mind and the strength to sustain its purity. Amen."*
- Congratulate the group on their progress and provide the Homework Assignment.

HOMEWORK ASSIGNMENT

Have participants read Chapter 8/Review, in the Workbook/Journal on pages 85-87 , and answer questions #1-10, on pages 87-89.

Also, have participants start Journal Entry #8 - Writing Assignment on page 92 in the Workbook/Journal.

Lesson Plan – Session #16/Changing Our "Stinking Thinking"

GOAL: **Enlighten participants on the importance of their perception of events and circumstances.**
Teach participants how to control their thoughts and train their minds to think positive.

- Open your session by having participants read aloud, together, the prayer on page 108, in the text:

    "God, You are great, kind and merciful. Thank You for exposing me to the truth of the importance of my thinking. Today I desire to change my thoughts that have adversely affected my mind. Help me to fill my mind with positive thoughts. Send positive people into my life who can support and encourage me. Alert me when my thoughts are off track, and help me to quickly change them. I thank You now for a new mind and the strength to sustain its purity. Amen."

- Have participants read Chapter 8/Review on pages pages 85-87, in the Workbook/Journal.
- Then, have participants answer questions #1-10, on pages 87-89, in the Workbook/Journal. Allow questions to be open for discussion.
- Have participants review the Chapter example on pages 103-106, in the text.
- Then, have participants answer questions #1-5 on pages 90-91, in the Workbook/Journal. Allow questions to be open for discussion.
- Have participants complete Journal Entry #8 on page 92, in the Workbook/Journal.
- Ask volunteers to share their journal entries. Allow the group to discuss each entry.

- Congratulate the group on their success, and provide the Homework Assignment.

HOMEWORK ASSIGNMENT

Have participants read Chapter 9: Managing Your Emotions, in the text.

Lesson Plan – Session #17/Managing Your Emotions

GOAL: Help participants identify their feelings and emotions and understand their purpose.

- Have participants take turns reading, aloud, Chapter 9: Managing Your Emotions on pages 111-121, in the text.
- Open discussion: what are the participants' thoughts and feelings about this chapter?
- Have participants complete Handout #15, located in the back of this book. Questions on this handout include:
    1) What main points or new revelations did you gain from Chapter 9?
    2) What is the key to managing our emotions?
    3) Is having feelings and emotions always bad? Why or why not?
    4) Describe in a few sentences a situation that caused you to fear. How did you react?
    5) Describe in a few sentences a situation that caused you to worry. How did you react?
    6) Describe in a few sentences a situation that caused you to doubt. How did you react?
    7) Describe in a few sentences a situation that caused you to become depressed, and how you reacted.
    8) Describe in a few sentences a situation that caused you to become angry, and how you reacted.
    9) Describe in a few sentences a situation that caused you to become jealous, and how you reacted.
    10) Describe in a few sentences, a situation that caused you to take revenge, and how you reacted.

11) What negative emotions do you need to address?
12) How will you overcome these emotions?

- Have participants take turns answering the questions on Handout #15. Allow each question to be open for discussion.
- Close your session by having participants read aloud, together, the prayer on page 120, in the text:

    "God, I thank You for exposing to me the importance of managing my emotions. I come to You today seeking Your help, strength, and guidance. Enable me to learn how to control my emotions. Guide me with Your wisdom. Allow me to see Your purpose and plan for my life. Illuminate the good in every situation. Allow me to see it and reflect on it in my thinking, regardless of what I am experiencing. Shower me with Your love and erase all my fears, worries and doubts. Show me my strengths, gifts and talents, and give me the confidence to obtain my goals and my purpose in life. Keep me protected from all evil, hurt, and harm. Shine Your light on me. Transform my heart and mind, and lead me into Your expected results. Amen."

- Congratulate the group on their progress, and provide the Homework Assignment.

HOMEWORK ASSIGNMENT

Read Chapter 9/Review in the Workbook/Journal on pages 95-98. Answer the questions #1-10 on pages 98-100.

Start working on Journal Entry #9 - Writing Assignment, on page 103, in the Workbook/Journal.

Lesson Plan – Session #18/Managing Your Emotions

GOAL: Enlighten participants about the detriments of holding on to anger, fear, worry and doubt.
Teach participants how to cope with and overcome all negative emotions.

- Start the group by having participants read aloud, together, the prayer on page 120, in the text:

    "God, I thank You for exposing to me the importance of managing my emotions. I come to You today seeking Your help, strength, and guidance. Enable me to learn to control my emotions. Guide me with Your wisdom. Cause me to see Your purpose and plan for my life. Illuminate the good in every situation. Allow me to see it and reflect on it in my thinking, regardless of what I am experiencing. Shower me with Your love and erase all my fears, worries and doubts. Show me my strengths, gifts and talents, and give me the confidence to obtain my goals and my purpose in life. Keep me protected from all evil, hurt, and harm. Shine Your light on me. Transform my heart and mind, and lead me into Your expected results. Amen."

- Have participants take turns reading, aloud, Chapter 9/Review, in the Workbook/Journal on pages 95-98.
- Then, have participants answer questions #1-10 on pages 98-100. Open questions for group discussion.
- Have participants read the Example Section, in the Workbook/Journal, on pages 100-101.
- Then, have participants answer questions #1-5, on pages 102-103, in the Workbook/Journal. Open questions for group discussion.

- Based on the journal entries that participants prepared for Homework on page 103 in the Workbook/Journal, have participants complete pages 106-107 and write three ways they can diffuse their negative emotions and three ways they can sustain their positive emotions for longer periods of time. This exercise is listed in Journal Entry #9, on page 103, in the Workbook/Journal. Open questions and journal entries to discussion.
- Congratulate participants on their success, and provide the Homework Assignment.

HOMEWORK ASSIGNMENT

Have participants read Chapter 10: Learning to Care for "Self," in the text.

Lesson Plan – Session #19/Learning to Care for "Self"

GOAL: Help participants develop inner self-pride and self-esteem by enlightening them on the truth of who they are, so they become in tune with "self."
Introduce participants to the importance of caring for "self."

- Start the group session by asking participants the following questions, open for discussion:
    1) What new discoveries have you made about yourself?
    2) As you've applied the techniques and utilized the information we have learned thus far, have you noticed a change in the way you view yourself and your circumstances?
    3) What areas do you feel still need improvement?
- Have participants take turns reading, aloud Chapter 10: Learning to Care for "Self," on pages 123-133. Stop on page 127, as instructed in the text, and have participants complete the self-analysis chart on pages 110-112 in the Workbook/Journal. Then, continue to have participants take turns reading, aloud, the rest of the chapter.
- Open discussion: what are the participants' thoughts and feelings about this chapter?
- Have participants complete Handout #16, located in the back of this book. Questions on this handout include:
    1) After reading Chapter 10 in the text, do you feel that you have adequately cared for yourself in the past? Why or why not?
    2) Why is caring for yourself important?
    3) What can you do right away to begincaring for "self?"
    4) Do you set boundaries in your relationships with others? Why or why not?

5) When we begin to protect, admire and love ourselves, how do our lives change?
- Have participants take turns answering the questions on Handout #16. Allow each question to be open for discussion.
- Close your session by having participants read the prayer on page 132, in the text:

    "God, I thank You for showing me the beauty and the importance of 'self.' I ask that You help me to recognize my full potential within. Empower me to see myself from Your perspective. Teach me how to love, care, and appreciate 'self.' When I fall short in these areas, gently nudge me and remind me to care for 'self.' Give me the strength I need to sustain that care. Increase my self-esteem and confidence daily as I embark on this journey of restoration. Lead me and guide me into Your perfect will and plan. Amen."

- Congratulate participants on their progress and provide the Homework Assignment.

HOMEWORK ASSIGNMENT

Have participants read Chapter 10/Review in the Workbook/Journal on pages 109-110, and answer questions #1-9 on pages 113-115. Also, have participants start Journal Entry #10 on page 115, in the Workbook/Journal.

Lesson Plan – Session #20/Learning to Care for "Self"

GOAL: Teach participants how to tap into their inner joy by evaluating the things in life they enjoy and things that make them unhappy.

Enlighten participants on ways they can protect "self" and reward "self."

- Start your session by having participants read aloud, together, the prayer on page 132, in the text:

    God, I thank You for showing me the beauty and the importance of 'self.' I ask that You help me to recognize my full potential within. Empower me to see myself from Your perspective. Teach me how to love, care, and appreciate 'self.' When I fall short in these areas, gently nudge me and remind me to care for 'self.' Give me the strength I need to sustain that care. Increase my self-esteem and confidence daily as I embark on this journey of restoration. Lead me and guide me into Your perfect will and plan. Amen."

- Have participants take turns reading aloud Chapter 10/Review in the Workbook/Journal on pages 109-110.
- Then, have participants take turns answering questions #1-9 on pages 113-115. Allow these questions to be open for discussion.
- Have participants take turns reading aloud the example on Handout #17.
- Then, have participants answer the questions 1-5 on Handout #17 that relate to the example. Allow these questions to be open for discussion.
- Have participants complete Journal Entry #10, on page 115 in the Workbook/Journal.

- Ask for participants to share their journal entries. Allow each entry to be open for discussion.
- Congratulate participants on their success, and provide the Homework Assignment.

HOMEWORK ASSIGNMENT

Have participants read Chapter 11: Alternatives to Crime, in the text.

Lesson Plan – Session #21/Alternatives to Crime

GOAL: Enlighten participants on the need to become responsible and mature, recognizing there are always consequences from criminal behavior.
Help participants assess their skill sets and talents.

- Have participants take turns reading aloud Chapter 11 in the text on pages 135-142.
- Open discussion: what are the participants' thoughts and feelings about this chapter?
- Have participants complete Handout #18, located in the back of this book. Questions in this handout include:
    1) What consequences have you suffered because of your participation in criminal activities?
    2) What could you have done differently and how would your life be different if you did not make the mistake of participating in crime?
    3) Can a person succeed if they live a criminal lifestyle? Why or why not?
    4) How can we turn our skill sets and talents into promoting a good, wholesome, integral lifestyle?
    5) Have you matured during this time of incarceration? Why or Why not?
    6) What do you excel at doing?
    7) What can you do for extended periods of time that brings you satisfaction?
    8) What activities do you do that keep your adrenaline pumping and give you a natural high?
    9) What is your dream occupation?
    10) What goals would you like to achieve when you are released from prison?

- Have participants take turns answering the questions on Handout #19. Allow each question to be open for discussion.
- Close the session by having participants read aloud, together, the prayer on page 142, in the text:

    "God, I thank You for opening my mind to alternatives to crime. I deeply desire to change my old ways and habits. I ask for Your guidance along this journey. Help me to discover my gifts and talents. Illuminate the areas that I am strongest in. Send people and resources that will help promote my cause. Keep me from all evil and temptation. Help me to stay focused on my goals and not be distracted or go off track. I thank You now for Your wisdom, knowledge and direction. Amen."

- Congratulate your group on their progress and provide the Homework Assignment.

HOMEWORK ASSIGNMENT

Have participants read Chapter 11/Review in the Workbook/Journal, on pages 117-118. Then, answer questions #1-5 on pages 118-119, in the Workbook/Journal. Also, have participants start Journal Entry #11, on page 123, in the Workbook/Journal.

Lesson Plan – Session #22/Alternatives to Crime

GOAL: Enlighten participants on the resources and options available for ex-felons.
Provide information to participants explaining how they can develop their skill sets and talents, and how they can find occupations and training to live as a productive citizen.

- Start the session by having participants read aloud, together, the prayer on page 142, in the text:

  "God, I thank You for opening my mind to alternatives to crime. I deeply desire to change my old ways and habits. I ask for Your guidance along this journey. Help me to discover my gifts and talents. Illuminate the areas where I excel. Send people and resources to me that will help promote my cause. Keep me from all evil and temptation. Help me to stay focused on my goals and not be distracted or go off track. I thank You now for Your wisdom, knowledge and direction. Amen."

- Have participants read aloud, together, Chapter 11/Review on pages 117-118, in the Workbook/Journal.
- Then, have participants answer questions #1-5 on pages 118-119, in the Workbook/Journal. Allow questions to be open for discussion.
- Have participants reread the chapter examples, in the text, on pages 136-139.
- Then, have the participants answer questions #1-10 on pages 120-122, in the Workbook/Journal. Allow questions to be open for discussion.
- Have participants complete Journal Entry #11-Writing Assignment, on page 123, in the Workbook/Journal. Ask volunteers to share their Journal entries. Allow each entry to be open for discussion.
- Congratulate the group on their progress, and provide their Homework Assignment.

HOMEWORK ASSIGNMENT

Have participants read Chapter 12: Each Day Becoming a Better "Self," in the text.

Lesson Plan – Session #23/Each Day Becoming a Better "Self"

GOAL: Enlighten participants on how to apply the techniques and strategies learned in the VOC program to everyday life. Teach participants how to perform a continuous self-assessment throughout the day.

- Have participants take turns reading, aloud, Chapter 12: Each Day Becoming a Better "Self" on pages 143-150 in the text.
- Open discussion: what are the participants' thoughts and feelings about this chapter?
- Have participants answer questions #1-10 on pages 126-129 in the Workbook/Journal. Allow questions to be open for discussion.
- Have participants read the Example Section, in the Workbook/Journal, on pages 129-130.
- Then, have participants answer questions #1-5 on pages 130-131, in the Workbook/Journal. Allow questions to be open for discussion.
- Close the group by asking participants to read the prayer, together, on page 149 in the text.
    > *"God, I thank You for helping me recognize how I can become a better 'self.' Help me to apply these techniques to my life, and enlighten me with new techniques and strategies that can help me improve myself. Empower me to become the best me I can possibly be! My desire is to make You proud. Strengthen me, lead me, and guide me all the days of my life. Amen."*
- Congratulate participants on their progress and provide the Homework Assignment.

HOMEWORK ASSIGNMENT

Have participants read Chapter 12/Review on pages 125-126, in the Workbook/Journal. Also, have participants start Journal Entry #12, on pages 132-133 in the Workbook/Journal.

Lesson Plan – Session #24/Each Day Becoming a Better "Self"

GOAL: Enlighten participants on the power of visualization, helping them to see themselves as successful.
Help participants develop a plan for self-improvement based on the strategies and techniques learned in the VOC series.

Start the session by having participants read aloud, together, the prayer on page 149, in the text:

> *"God, I thank You for helping me recognize how I can become a better 'self.' Help me to apply these techniques to my life, and enlighten me with new techniques and strategies that can help me improve myself. Empower me to become the best me I can possibly be! My desire is to make You proud. Strengthen me, lead me, and guide me all the days of my life. Amen."*

- Have participants take turns reading, aloud, Chapter 12/Review on pages 125-126, in the Workbook/Journal.
- Open discussion on what are the participants' thoughts and feelings about this chapter.
- Have participants complete Journal Entry #12 on pages 132-133 in the Workbook/Journal.
- Ask participants to share their entries. Allow each entry to be open for discussion.
- Then, give participants the Final Exam, located in the back of this book.
- Congratulate each participant for their success in completing the course. Encourage participants to continue onto the next step in the journey to restoration, *Permission to Dream*.

UNLOCKING THE PRISON DOORS

Name _____

Register # _____

Date _____

HANDOUT #1

Introduction to Unlocking the Prison Doors

Welcome aboard! You've just embarked on a wonderful journey to "Mission Change." This is not the usual journey. It will take courage and tenacity to complete this mission, but your efforts will be well worth it! You stand to gain much!

Imprisonment can be a difficult experience. No one wants to be trapped, lost and lonely, away from those we know and love. To many, imprisonment may be the most difficult experience you have ever encountered. Many believe it is just a waste of time, but it doesn't have to be! This time of imprisonment can be a gift. It is up to us to take our adversities and turn them into opportunities for advancement. The VOC series will help you do just that. Let's use this time wisely and grow, working on our greatest asset, which is "self."

Before we begin you must be committed to embracing this opportunity and open your mind, preparing yourself to tap into the power of "self."

Are you ready to begin? Let's move ahead. Don't look back! Roll up your sleeves and answer the following questions based on what you've learned thus far:

1) What do you think you can gain from this course?

_____
_____
_____
_____

2) How does this course differ from typical group sessions?

_____
_____
_____
_____

3) Are you willing to be open-minded as you embark on this new journey, "Mission Change?"

_____
_____
_____
_____
_____

4) What supplies will you need during this course?

_____
_____
_____
_____
_____

5) What requirements must you fulfill to complete this course?

_____
_____
_____
_____
_____
_____

Name _____

Register # _____

Date _____

HANDOUT #2
Learning to Surrender

One of the most difficult things in life to do is to surrender. As humans we want control over our lives and what happens to us each day. The truth is, tomorrow is not promised to any of us. Therefore, we must live life as meaningfully as possible.

We are here at this time, at this place, for a reason. It's time to reevaluate our lives, our lifestyles and our values. It is important that we don't continue to make the same mistakes of the past. It's time to grow up and to change.

Take a moment and read the poem, "A Prisoner's Cry," on pages 10-13 in the text. Stop and reflect. Then answer the questions below:

1) What similarities do you have to the women's lives mentioned in the poem?

    _____
    _____
    _____
    _____
    _____

2) What events in life led these women astray? Can you relate? Why or why not?

    _____
    _____
    _____
    _____
    _____

3) What choices did these women make? Why were these poor choices?

　

4) What does the poet suggest women do if they want to change?

　

5) Are you ready to surrender and open your life to change? Why or why not?

Name _____

Register # _____

Date _____

HANDOUT #3

Accepting Help from Our "Higher Power"

It is important to know that during this journey we are not alone. Regardless of our circumstances or our situation, there is help! That help has always been available to us. We must tap in!

Many of us were busy in the world, caught up in doing our own thing. We often disregarded that still small voice within that tried to lead us in the way that we ought to go. Now we have time to stop and listen. Our obstacles have led us to the Solution. Our "Higher Power" wishes to take the lead and guide us through this journey. Prosperity begins by developing a relationship with the Almighty, the all-powerful God that lives within us. After reading Chapter 2, in the text, answer the following questions:

1) Has this chapter changed your perception about God or the need for a "Higher Power?" Why or why not?

_____

_____

_____

_____

_____

2) Based on this reading has your perception of your current situation changed? Why or why not?

_____

_____

_____

_____

3) Do you believe God allowed your current circumstances of imprisonment for a greater purpose? Why or why not?

_____

_____

_____

_____

Based on the example in Chapter 2, on pages 22-24 in the text, answer the following questions:

4) Can you relate to Tracy or have you seen others in prison experience the same hardships as Tracy did with her husband? Explain.

_____

_____

_____

_____

5) What did God allow Tracy's hardships to reveal to her?

_____

_____

_____

_____

6) Why do you think Sam changed when Tracy became incarcerated? Did he ever really love her? Why or why not?

_____
_____
_____
_____
_____
_____

7) What good came out of Tracy's incarceration?

_____
_____
_____
_____
_____
_____

8) How did Tracy benefit from developing a relationship with her "Higher Power?"

_____
_____
_____
_____
_____
_____

Name _____

Register # _____

Date _____

HANDOUT #4

Getting to the Root of the Problem—"Who Am I?"

During the journey to restoration, it is essential that we look back at the childhood experiences that influenced how we developed into who we are now.

Stop and take a moment to reflect. Think about how life began, when you were a sweet innocent little girl, undefiled by life's negative influences. Step into that moment and experience the feelings you had back then.

As you recapture those moments in your mind, answer the following questions:

1) Did you receive the love, care, and the compassion you needed as a child? Explain.

   _____
   _____
   _____
   _____
   _____

2) Did you feel safe and secure as a child? Why or why not?

   _____
   _____
   _____
   _____
   _____

3) Were you ever violated sexually or physically? Explain.

_____
_____
_____
_____

4) Did you ever experience verbal abuse? Explain.

_____
_____
_____
_____

5) Were both of your parents there to raise you? Explain.

_____
_____
_____
_____

6) Did your life turn out to be similar to those whom you were around growing up? Explain.

_____
_____
_____
_____

Name _____

Register # _____

Date _____

HANDOUT #5

Getting to the Root of the Problem—"Who Am I?"

It's time to dig deep and do some soul searching. Instead of being the person others desired you to be or the person you thought you needed to be to please others, discover who you really are. Take a moment to reflect. Think about your life and what you would like to accomplish. Then, answer the questions below:

1) How do you currently feel about yourself? Why?

   _____
   _____
   _____
   _____
   _____

2) What can you do to improve yourself?

   _____
   _____
   _____
   _____
   _____

3) How difficult will this be to accomplish?

_____
_____
_____
_____

4) How do you treat others?

_____
_____
_____
_____

5) Would you like others to treat you that way?

_____
_____
_____
_____

6) How strong are the relationships that you have developed with others? Explain.

_____
_____
_____
_____

7) Are these relationships positive? Why or why not?

8) What do you like to do in your spare time?

9) Are these activities productive? Why or why not?

10) What other productive activities do you think you should participate in?

11) What are your goals in life?

_____
_____
_____
_____
_____

12) What steps will it take to achieve these goals?

_____
_____
_____
_____
_____
_____

Name _____

Register # _____

Date _____

HANDOUT #6

Getting to the Root of the Problem– "Who Am I?"

CODEPENDENCY

A common issue that many inmates struggle with is codependency. Many of our biggest fears center on being alone. Therefore, we do whatever it takes to please and control others, hoping they will stay with us and journey together with us through life.

In this season it is important to learn how to be alone, how to tap into the joy and satisfaction within and discover how to be fearless, trusting that God will always be present with us and make provisions for us. As we become confident in self, we begin to soar! We know who we are, our value and what our purpose is here on Earth.

Therefore, we no longer fear being alone. We no longer try to control others, and we no longer allow others to influence us or control us. Instead, we take control over our lives, and we focus on our biggest asset, which is "self." The goal during this journey is to become free from the influence of other people, places and things. Instead of placing value in external things, we begin to find value in ourselves. Therefore, we are empowered!

It's time that we wake up and see the light. I'm going to share with you an example of a dependent behavior in prison. My prayer is that this example will shine light on the detriments of codependency, as well as shed light on issues that many of us deal with.

Example

Camille is a very pretty, talented girl who grew up in Columbia, South Carolina. Camille led her high school as the Student Body President. She won the crown as Miss Teen South Carolina, and she aced all her classes. In the eyes of everyone else, Camille had it going on. Despite her victories, Camille didn't believe she had achieved enough. Camille had a brother who always teased her and called her ugly. Subconsciously, Camille agreed with her brother's false remarks and fought deeply with her inner self-esteem.

If someone wasn't complimenting Camille, she did not feel good. Therefore, she always sought the esteem of others. Camille tried her best to please people. She thought that if she made them happy, they would like her and stay with her. Camille loved to be surrounded by others who would praise her and cheer her on.

One day Camille met a cute boy named Brian. Camille tried to get his attention, but Brian wasn't interested. Brian had it going on. He owned a local tire shop in their town, and he was also one of the town's top drug suppliers.

Camille became viciously angry as Brian refused to acknowledge her presence. One day, she went to his tire shop in her most provocative outfit and propositioned Brian. "Yeah, I know you can't handle a girl like me. I'm too independent for you, cause I'm about my money," Camille said as she flirted with Brian in a seductive manner.

That day, Camille caught Brian's attention and he put her right to work. Brian convinced Camille to start trafficking drugs for him, and Camille became one of the best workers he ever had. She wanted to please Brian so badly that she went above and beyond the call of duty. It's no surprise that when Brian asked her to start prostituting for him she also agreed. Camille would do anything to keep Brian happy, even if it meant endangering herself.

The Feds began a sting operation on Brian and, of course, Camille, as his top employee, got caught up. She received a three-point enhancement for a leadership role in his drug operation and was sentenced to fifteen years in federal prison.

Camille was devastated. She couldn't believe how her life had deteriorated. She accepted that life was over and looked for a way to cope in prison.

Although Camille was not gay, she latched on to a girl named Pam in Federal Prison. Pam had masculine features and for the most part looked like a man. Camille passionately pursued Pam. She used all her commissary money to buy Pam gifts. She washed Pam's clothes, cooked her food, cleaned her cell, and did anything else she thought would please Pam.

Pam accepted Camille's gifts, yet she pursued other women on the prison compound.

Life in prison became chaotic for Camille. In the street, Camille was not a fighter, yet in prison she fought almost every other week. Camille found herself caught in a web with Pam and all of Pam's women.

Camille didn't care; she knew she would be with Pam for life. The constant chaos went on for four years, until it was time for Pam's release. Pam had no real family support, so Camille coerced her mom to buy Pam an outfit to wear, put money in Pam's account and purchased a plane ticket back home for Pam.

Camille was sad to see her true love leave prison, but the two girls promised to stay in touch. Pam told Camille she would write her every day and send Camille money, which brightened Camille's outlook.

On the way out the prison door, Pam gave Camille her telephone number and address. The two girls hugged passionately as Pam exited the prison doors.

A week went by and Camille missed Pam. She put Pam's telephone number on her phone list and rushed to the phone to call Pam. Camille dialed the number and heard a recording. The telephone number was disconnected. Camille didn't give up; she waited patiently to hear from Pam. Pam never reached out to Camille. In Pam's mind the relationship was over. The relationship was just something to do while she was in prison.

Pam went home and reestablished a relationship with her daughter's father, whom she is currently cheating on with his good friend and another girl she met in prison.

Questions

1) What were Camille's major issues that made her vulnerable?

2) How did these issues affect Camille's life?

3) How would life be different for Camille if she loved and cared for self?

4) Did Camille's efforts to please her lovers really control them? Why or why not?

5) Did Camille have the ability to change Brian and Pam? Why or why not?

_____
_____
_____
_____
_____

Review pages 37-41 in the text on codependency and answer the following questions:

1) Describe codependency in your own words.

_____
_____
_____
_____
_____

2) Why do people become codependent on others?

_____
_____
_____
_____
_____

3) Is codependency healthy? Why or why not?

_____
_____
_____
_____
_____

4) Give an example of codependent behavior in prison.

5) Why do codependent people falsely believe they are in control or possess power over another?

6) Can we control people? Why or why not?

7) What is the solution to codependency?

8) How do we develop healthy boundaries in relationships?

9) What is "disabling" a person?

10) What is "enabling" a person?

Name _____

Register # _____

Date _____

HANDOUT #7

Acknowledging Our Shortcomings

One of the most difficult things in life to do is to acknowledge our inadequacies. Everyone wants to feel capable and to be right. Therefore, we hide the truth of our faults and the actions we take that are not correct.

Staying in denial is dangerous. It does not allow us the room we need to grow and become better people. We do not have to remain in denial! We have a plan. Let's peel off our mask and discover our failings, so we can fix them.

You are not alone in this journey. You have help and support along the way. Be honest with yourself and strive to become the best that you can possibly be. You are a winner!

Based on your self-analysis, after reading Chapter 4 in the text and doing the exercises in Chapter 4 in the Workbook/Journal, answer the following questions:

1) Who Am I? (List both the positive and negative characteristics you discovered through the Moral Inventory of Weaknesses and Good Character Traits. Utilize the evaluation grids in the Workbook/Journal on page 40 and page 45.)

_____

_____

_____

_____

_____

_____

2) Who do I wish to become? (Think about the areas you want to improve in and write out the characteristics you desire to have.)

Name _____

Register # _____

Date _____

HANDOUT #8
Acknowledging Our Shortcomings

NEGATIVE RELATIONSHIPS

If you were to conduct a poll of how many women landed in prison because of bad relationships, the results would astound you! From lovers, parents, friends and relatives to associates, many of us were led astray. Their values became our values. Therefore, we began to believe that our actions were acceptable. "Everyone's doing it, so I'll do it too," became our reasoning. Many of us learned the hard way: "You are the company you keep."

We no longer need to stay stagnant. We can dust off the defilements of the past and soar in life. Our victory begins when we make changes in the company we choose to keep.

Let's take a moment and explore how relationships can affect our lives.

Example

Judy was a popular girl, growing up in Houston, Texas. She was a cheerleader and hung out with the "in" crowd. Judy believed her worth was based on how others around her viewed her life. Therefore, she became caught up in doing what pleased the crowd.

Judy's mom was a strict disciplinarian. Judy had to be a good girl in the sight of her mom, yet when she went to school she became a entirely different person. Judy would leave her house in long skirts and change in the school bathroom into short, skimpy skirts.

Lured in by the crowd, Judy tired of hiding who she really was. Convinced by her friend Shannon, she decided to pack up everything she had and move to Miami, Florida.

Shannon and Judy hooked up with some new friends and began to strip at a local nightclub, where they made money hand over fist. Judy began to live the good life! Sex, money, drugs and men became the norm. Judy felt as though she was living it up. There was no turning back for Judy. In Judy's eyes, she had the acceptance of all those around her, those who she thought were cool, and for her, that was all that mattered.

One night at the club, Judy met a baller named Harold. He spent over a thousand dollars tipping Judy for dancing for him. Judy was on a high as the dollars flooded in. She was determined to make Harold her own, and she did!

Harold made Judy his girlfriend and forced her to quit her job at the strip club. Barely legal, she had no skills that could sustain her the way her dancing did at the club. Therefore, she convinced Harold to let her in on his gun and drug trafficking business. Judy traveled around the country buying and selling drugs. Too bad one of her top clients was an undercover federal agent. Not only did she get caught up in the sting, so did Harold. They were both sentenced to ten years in federal prison.

Judy was devastated when she was locked up. For the first time in years, she called her mom, and her mom came to her rescue. Judy cried for days after her visit with her mom in prison. She suddenly realized how stupid her behavior was and how much her mom loved her.

In prison, Judy joined the prison psychology group and began focusing on her past issues. She met a lady named Debra who was an attorney in prison for insider trading. Debra became Judy's mentor. She encouraged Judy to earn her GED and helped her enroll in college courses through correspondence. The two women spent hours talking. Debra shared her lifestyle, which fascinated Judy. Judy aspired to become as successful as Debra once was.

As a result, Judy was released from prison, moved to California and became a lawyer.

Today she helps federal inmates overturn their convictions.

1) Did Shannon have a good influence on Judy's life? Why or why not?

2) Why did Judy leave home? Was her decision to leave good or bad? Why?

3) Did Harold have a good influence on Judy's life? Why or why not?

4) Why was Judy attracted to Shannon and Harold?

5) Did Debra have a good influence on Judy's life? Why or why not?

_____

_____

_____

_____

_____

6) What does this example illustrate about destructive relationships?

_____

_____

_____

_____

_____

_____

Name _____

Register # _____

Date _____

HANDOUT #9

Accepting Responsibility for Our Actions

As we journey on the road to restoration, it is important that we acknowledge our past wrongdoings and accept responsibility for our actions. We can no longer blame others for the choices we have made. Even if we were influenced strongly by others or misled, we ultimately decided to accept the advice of another. Thus, we must accept responsibility for our wrong choices.

When we don't accept responsibility, we remain stagnant. We cannot move ahead if we stay trapped in our past. Today we have a choice. We can choose to grow. Growth occurs when we acknowledge the truth of our past, make the necessary adjustments and move ahead in life. Freedom begins when we embrace this process.

Are you ready to open the doors that have been holding you bound? Take a deep breath and be honest with yourself. What could you have done differently? Take a moment to consider this. Then, answer the following questions:

1) After reading Chapter 5 in the text, describe in your own words what adverse actions you took that led to your imprisonment.

_____

_____

_____

_____

_____

_____

2) What role did you play in these actions?

   _____
   _____
   _____
   _____
   _____
   _____
   _____
   _____
   _____
   _____

3) What are the consequences you must now endure because of your behavior?

   _____
   _____
   _____
   _____
   _____
   _____
   _____
   _____
   _____
   _____

4) Do you regret your decision to take part in this behavior? Why or why not?

   _____
   _____
   _____
   _____

_____
_____
_____
_____
_____
_____

5) Do you fully accept responsibility for your wrongdoings? Explain.

_____
_____
_____
_____
_____
_____
_____
_____
_____
_____

Name _____

Register # _____

Date _____

HANDOUT #10
Accepting Responsibility for Our Actions

A part from accepting responsibility is acknowledging those who have suffered because of our adverse actions. It is easy to get caught up in the "Woe is me" syndrome, believing we are victims ourselves. As a victim, we are unable to clearly identify those who are also left to suffer because of our mistakes.

It is essential in this season that we change our perspective and honestly consider the hardships of others caused by our adverse behavior. When we truly recognize our victims and their plight, it becomes easier to accept responsibility for our wrongdoings.

Therefore, it is time to view our crimes from the outside, looking in. Who has suffered because of our actions? Take a moment to honestly examine your answer, and complete the questions below:

1) Identify the victims who have suffered because of your crime.

_____

_____

_____

_____

_____

_____

_____

_____

_____

2) In what ways have each of these victims suffered?

_____
_____
_____
_____
_____
_____
_____
_____
_____
_____

Name _____

Register # _____

Date _____

HANDOUT #11
Closing the Doors to Shame and Guilt

Now that we have honestly evaluated our wrongdoings and have accepted responsibility for our actions, it is important that we rid ourselves of shame and guilt.

Guilt and shame serve a purpose. It is to awaken our conscience to our wrongdoings. After we acknowledge our faults, we must change our course. Then, let our negative feelings go! We must never hold on to shame and guilt. If we do, these emotions can destroy us both physically and mentally. Therefore, we must release them!

Take a moment to evaluate your life to determine if you harbor any hidden shame and guilt. During this journey we must dig deep and root out any defilement that can keep us down.

Are you ready to become victorious? Be honest with yourself, evaluate your life, and answer the questions below:

1) Describe shame in your own words.

_____
_____
_____
_____
_____
_____
_____

2) Describe guilt in your own words.

_____
_____
_____
_____
_____

3) Stop and analyze your life. Are you currently holding on to any shame or guilt? Explain.

_____
_____
_____
_____
_____

4) Why is it important to rid yourself of shame and guilt?

_____
_____
_____
_____
_____

5) How can you begin to heal and become emotionally healthy?

_____
_____
_____
_____
_____
_____

Name _____

Register # _____

Date _____

HANDOUT #12
Closing the Doors to Shame and Guilt

Self-Forgiveness

Many of us have wallowed in the undercurrents of life because we have not forgiven ourselves. We've examined our lives and acknowledged our mistakes. Then, we beat ourselves up, over and over again, for making poor choices. Many of us have even internalized our feelings and harbor them deep within. This has caused us to secretly hate ourselves. Instead of feeling as though we made a mistake, we falsely believe we are a mistake. These feelings are deadly. We must not let the past determine our future. We can take hold of tomorrow by simply making a choice to change.

Today we can choose to acknowledge our faults, to learn from them. Then, let them go! Today we can choose to be successful. Today we can become a victor and no longer a victim of our own self-hate. Today we possess the power to succeed, simply by our choices! Do you choose to overcome? Forgive yourself!!!

Self-forgiveness is an active determination. That means you must purposefully eliminate all negative thoughts and feelings about your past and actively pursue a wonderful future.

Take a breath and get ready to let the past go! Move ahead and mindfully answer the questions below:

1) Can you change the past? Why or why not?

_____

_____

_____

_____

2) Does your past dictate your future? Why or why not?

_____
_____
_____
_____

3) If you hate yourself, how will others treat you? Explain.

_____
_____
_____
_____
_____

4) How can you take hold of your future?

_____
_____
_____
_____
_____

5) What good do you hold inside that can be shared here on earth that would please your "Higher Power?"

_____
_____
_____
_____
_____

Name _____

Register # _____

Date _____

HANDOUT #13
Forgiving Others Who Have Wronged Us

Many of us have suffered from hurt, pain and disappointment triggered by the adverse actions of others. Our internal pain has caused us to build walls of protection with hopes that no one else will be able to cause us any further grief.

Many of us have tried to bury our past. Because certain events were so painful, we try our best to block them from our minds. Even through our blockage many of us have harbored the ill feelings for those who have hurt us. Some of those feelings have even escalated into a deep hatred. As a result, we have become handcuffed to those who abused us. Regardless of our efforts to forget the events, our ill feelings towards our abusers have kept us bound.

We no longer have to stay handcuffed to those who hurt us. We hold the power to break free, through our ability to forgive.

Take a moment to go back and pinpoint the events that allowed your unforgiveness to settle in. Then, answer the questions below:

1) Write down the most significant events in your life that have caused you the most pain. (Summarize these events in a few sentences.)

_____

_____

_____

_____

_____

_____

_____

2) Write down the names of the individuals who hurt you as a result of these events.

___

3) Have you forgiven the individuals who hurt you? Why or why not?

___

Name _____

Register # _____

Date _____

HANDOUT #14
Changing Our "Stinking Thinking"

One of the biggest causes of adverse behavior is "stinking thinking." When we have the wrong mindset and mentality, we are led astray.

It is vital that we begin to change our thought patterns. Our thoughts determine our actions. Therefore, when we change our thoughts, we change our lives.

Begin to consider what you're thinking about. Examine your thoughts before you react. Measure the consequences before you make decisions that can impair your life.

Take a moment to reflect on the questions below. Then, answer each question as honestly as possible:

1) Describe in your own words the definition of "stinking thinking."

_____
_____
_____
_____
_____

2) Do you believe "stinking thinking" led you to prison? Why or why not?

_____
_____
_____
_____
_____

3) What can you do to rid yourself of "stinking thinking?"

_____
_____
_____
_____
_____

4) Give an example of positive thinking that you can use in your life.

_____
_____
_____
_____
_____

5) Do your thoughts determine your future? Why or why not?

_____
_____
_____
_____
_____
_____

Name _____

Register # _____

Date _____

HANDOUT #15
Managing Your Emotions

To take control over our lives, we must learn how to manage our emotions. We can no longer allow ourselves to be controlled by our feelings or the actions of others.

We master life when we learn the art of self-control. Therefore, we should do our best to maintain our composure, and not let negative emotions take command. We must monitor our thoughts and rid ourselves of all negativity. Through this process, we learn to overcome!

After reading Chapter 9, in the text, answer the following questions:

1) What main points of discovery or new revelations did you receive from Chapter 9?

_____
_____
_____
_____
_____

2) What is the key to managing our emotions?

_____
_____
_____
_____
_____
_____
_____

3) Is having feelings and emotions always wrong? Why or why not?

4) Describe in a few sentences a situation that caused you to fear. How did you react?

5) Describe in a few sentences a situation that caused you to worry. How did you react?

6) Describe in a few sentences a situation that caused you to doubt. How did you react?

7) Describe in a few sentences a situation that caused you to become depressed. How did you react?

___

8) Describe in a few sentences a situation that caused you to become angry. How did you react?

___

9) Describe in a few sentences a situation that caused you to become jealous. How did you react?

___

10) Describe in a few sentences a situation that caused you to take your own revenge. How did you react?

___

11) What negative emotions do you need to resolve? Explain.

_____
_____
_____
_____
_____

12) How will you overcome these emotions? Explain.

_____
_____
_____
_____
_____
_____

Name _____

Register # _____

Date _____

HANDOUT #16
Learning to Care for "Self"

One of the most rewarding experiences you can receive in life is learning to care for "self." During this journey we have learned that we no longer need to wait for others to do for us that which we can do for "self." We've learned how to become our own protector, lover and best friend. Therefore, we no longer rely on others to provide our happiness. Instead, we take control and create our own inner joy.

Each day we learn how to improve "self," and as we grow, we reward ourselves. We take time out to love and care for "self." As a result, we feel good inside and that goodness radiates into the universe commanding rewards to come our way. We've finally learned the secret! A good life comes through caring for "self."

Take a moment to read Chapter 10 in the text. Then, answer the following questions:

1) After reading Chapter 10 in the text, do you feel that you have adequately cared for yourself in the past? Why or why not?

_____
_____
_____
_____
_____
_____

2) Why is caring for yourself important?

_____
_____
_____
_____
_____

3) What can you do now to begin caring for "self?"

_____
_____
_____
_____
_____

4) Do you set boundaries in your relationships with others? Why or why not?

_____
_____
_____
_____
_____

5) When we begin to protect, admire and love ourselves, how do our lives change?

_____
_____
_____
_____
_____

Name _____

Register # _____

Date _____

HANDOUT #17
Learning to Care for "Self"

Example

Angel is a beautiful girl from Tulsa, Oklahoma, who just came home from serving a seven-year sentence for armed robbery.

Angel had a past history of domestic violence. Her husband, who was her childhood sweetheart, started abusing drugs, and he beat her. Angel loved her husband and gave him chance after chance to change. Not only didn't he stop his destructive behavior, he influenced Angel to accompany him on a bank robbery to obtain the money he needed to support his drug habit.

During Angel's imprisonment, she had the necessary time alone to reevaluate her life and her priorities. Angel received help from the prison psychologist, and for the first time she analyzed herself and her issues that led to imprisonment. The psychologist led Angel to regain her self-esteem and encouraged Angel to care for "self."

Prior to imprisonment, Angel had not received her high school diploma. After she met her husband in high school, she fell in love, got pregnant and dropped out of school. Angel's husband was a jealous man. He didn't want Angel to leave the house. He believed Angel should stay home and care for their son.

In prison, Angel went back to school and earned her GED. She also received her certification as a licensed cosmetologist.

In cosmetology classes, Angel became aware of her appearance. Angel loved how her new hair color and haircut made her look and feel. In the past Angel never made herself up, because her husband would accuse her of cheating on him.

Angel's makeover made her feel good about herself. She even began to wear makeup. As Angel felt better about herself, she discarded her depression and became vibrant. People began to compliment her, which reassured her, enforcing the idea that she was beautiful inside and out.

Not only did Angel keep her hair and makeup done, she developed a workout routine and lost over fifty pounds! "Watch out world, here I come," she would often say in the full-length mirror in the prison gym.

Recently, Angel arrived home from prison, and she has lived up to her words!

Angel was given a state grant through a convicted felon reentry program, and she opened her own beauty salon. Angel also participates in a program to do makeovers for cancer patients, and she loves it! On any given day, Angel's salon is filled with customers.

Angel is also dating a wonderful man. Today, she sets boundaries. She no longer allows anyone to take advantage of her or jeopardize her safety. By respecting herself, she causes others to respect her too.

Angel's life had a rocky start, but she took back control and turned it around. Today, Angel is successful!

1) Did Angel care for herself before her imprisonment? Explain.

_____
_____
_____
_____
_____

2) Why do you think Angel's husband continued to abuse her?

_____
_____
_____
_____
_____

3) How did Angel's life transform in prison?

4) What caused Angel's transformation?

5) How did Angel's transformation benefit her when she got out of prison?

Name _____

Register # _____

Date _____

HANDOUT #18
Alternatives to Crime

This journey helped us open our eyes and realize, "crime does not pay!" We now know whatever we gain from illegal means will not last. Ultimately, it will be taken away. Even if we take one step forward, eventually that crooked step will cause us to take two steps back. Therefore, we now realize the consequences for participating in illegal activities is not worthwhile.

During this journey, we learned how to tap into "self." In our self-discovery process, we discovered our gifts and talents as well as our likes and dislikes. These discoveries have led us on the path to finding our purpose.

This time around, we will be successful. The key to our success is finding a career that will be rewarding, as we engage in activities and make decisions in life that will result in our best!

Read Chapter 11, in the text, and answer the following questions:

1) What consequences have you suffered because of your participation in criminal activities?

_____

_____

_____

_____

_____

2) What could you have done differently, and how would your life be different if you did not make the mistake of participating in crime?

_____
_____
_____
_____

3) Can a person succeed if they live a criminal lifestyle? Why or why not?

_____
_____
_____
_____

4) How can we turn our skill sets and talents around to live a good, wholesome, integral lifestyle?

_____
_____
_____
_____

5) Have you matured during this time of incarceration? Why or why not?

_____
_____
_____
_____

6) What do you excel at doing?

_____
_____
_____
_____
_____

7) What can you do for extended periods of time that brings you satisfaction?

_____
_____
_____
_____
_____

8) What activities do you do that keeps your adrenaline pumping and gives you a natural high?

_____
_____
_____
_____
_____

9) What is your dream occupation?

_____
_____
_____
_____
_____

10) What goals would you like to achieve when you are released from prison?

_____
_____
_____
_____
_____

Name _____

Register # _____

Date _____

FINAL EXAMINATION

Unlocking the Prison Doors
Voices of Consequences Enrichment Series

Circle your answer to the following questions:

1) What does it mean to surrender?
    a) To give up attachment to results as we expect them.
    b) To let others hurt you and abuse you.
    c) To give up on life and quit.

2) What does surrendering require?
    a) Sleep.
    b) Willingness.
    c) Hard work.

3) Who is our "Higher Power?"
    a) A person we know.
    b) The rain.
    c) God as we know Him.

4) How can we receive help from God?
    a) By talking to a friend.
    b) By praying.
    c) By helping others.

5) People who aren't secure in their identities hide behind what?
    a) Their parents.
    b) Masks.
    c) A teacher.

6) In order to heal, become whole, and live life at our fullest potential, we must remove our
    a) hardships.
    b) clothes.
    c) masks.

7) Is childhood abuse the child's fault?
    a) Yes.
    b) No.
    c) Both.
8) Codependency is
    a) enlisting the support of others to challenge you.
    b) basing our self-worth on the ability to please someone else.
    c) relying on your parents to support you.
9) In order to heal we must acknowledge
    a) our friends.
    b) our shortcomings.
    c) we don't need help.
10) A blockage to healing is our
    a) problems.
    b) pain.
    c) denial.
11) Which group has all negative character traits?
    a) Generosity, kindness, patience.
    b) Jealousy, stubbornness, fear.
    c) Anger, humility, self-control.
12) Which group has all positive character traits?
    a) Generosity, kindness, patience.
    b) Jealousy, stubbornness, fear.
    c) Anger, humility, self-control.
13) Negative people
    a) lift us up.
    b) bring to light our faults.
    c) lead us astray.
14) Accepting responsibility is
    a) helping others.
    b) blaming others and remaining the same.
    c) the act of feeling remorse and correcting our wrongdoings.
15) In all crimes there is a
    a) victim.
    b) restitution.
    c) beneficiary.

16) What is shame?
    a) Admitting your wrongdoings.
    b) Feeling embarrassed.
    c) Saying sorry.
17) What is guilt?
    a) Feeling remorseful.
    b) Feeling sad.
    c) Feeling hurt.
18) Self-forgiveness is
    a) forgetting everything.
    b) letting the past go and loving "self."
    c) dressing up.
19) Why is unforgiveness dangerous?
    a) It causes anxiety.
    b) It produces bitterness and hate.
    c) It causes headaches.
20) Our abusers are also considered
    a) killers.
    b) victims.
    c) innocent.
21) What is "stinking thinking?"
    a) Smelly thoughts.
    b) Impaired, illogical thinking.
    c) Impatience.
22) What is the law of attraction?
    a) Bad thoughts grouped together.
    b) People who don't love themselves.
    c) Like attracts like.
23) What indicators let us know we are experiencing negative thoughts?
    a) Our feelings.
    b) Our tears.
    c) Our temperature.
24) What is the acronym for fear?
    a) False evidence appearing real.
    b) Frustrated escapes at restraint.
    c) Fundamental education always rocks.

25) Which group contains three negative emotions?
    a) Jealousy, hatred, kindness.
    b) Fear, worry, doubt.
    c) Happiness, joy, love.
26) How must we manage our emotions?
    a) Control the behavior of others.
    b) Control our thoughts.
    c) Control our environment.
27) What is caring for "self?"
    a) Always looking in the mirror.
    b) Frequently shopping.
    c) Being your own lover, protector and best friend.
28) What are boundaries?
    a) The lines we draw around our homes.
    b) The conditions we use to not allow others to take advantage.
    c) The time between meals.
29) How can we overcome the stigma of being an ex-con?
    a) Lie on our job application.
    b) Work hard and do the right thing.
    c) Be nice and smile.
30) Why are shortcuts dangerous?
    a) They are too easy.
    b) They cause anxiety.
    c) They lead to destruction.

Write a short essay about the actions you can take to become a better "self," and a more productive member of society? (Utilize the techniques and suggestions you learned during this course.)

About the Author

Jamila T. Davis, born and raised in Jamaica Queens, New York, is a motivational speaker and the creator of the Voices of Consequences Enrichment Series for incarcerated women. Through her powerful delivery, Davis illustrates the real-life lessons and consequences that result from poor choices. She also provides the techniques and strategies that she personally has utilized to dethrone negative thinking patterns, achieve emotional healing, and restoration and growth.

Davis is no stranger to triumphs and defeats. By the age of 25, she utilized her business savvy and street smarts to rise to the top of her field, becoming a lead go-to-person in the Hip-Hop Music Industry and a self-made millionaire through real estate investments. Davis lived a care-free lavish lifestyle, surrounded by rap stars, professional sports figures and other well known celebrities.

All seemed well until the thorn of materialism clouded Davis' judgments and her business shortcuts backfired, causing her self-made empire to crumble. Davis was convicted of bank fraud, for her role in a multi-million dollar bank fraud scheme, and sentenced to 12 1/2 years in federal prison.

Davis' life was in a great shambles as she faced the obstacle of imprisonment. While living in a prison cell, stripped of all her worldly possessions, and abandoned by most of her peers, she was forced to deal with the root of her dilemmas- her own inner self.

Davis searched passionately for answers and strategies to heal and regain her self-confidence, and to discover her life's purpose. She utilized her formal training from Lincoln University, in Philadelphia, Pennsylvania, along with her real-life post-incarceration experiences and documented her discoveries. Revealing the tools, techniques and strategies she used to heal, Davis composed a series of books geared to empower women. Davis' goal is to utilize her life experiences to uplift, inspire and empower her audience to achieve spiritual and emotional wholeness and become their very best, despite their dilemmas and past obstacles.

Voices International Publications Presents

Voices of CONSEQUENCES
ENRICHMENT SERIES
CREATED BY: JAMILA T. DAVIS

Volume #1-
Unlocking the
Prison Doors:
12 Points to Inner
Healing and
Restoration
ISBN: 978-09855807-0-4

Volume #2-
Permission to
Dream:
12 Points to Recapturing
Your Dreams and
Discovering Your Life's
Purpose
ISBN: 978-09855807-4-2

Volume #3-
Pursuit To A Greater "Self:"
12 Points to Developing Good
Character Traits and Healthy
Relationships
ISBN: 978-09855807-7-3

Purchase your copies today!

Visit us on the web @ www.vocseries.com, or write us at
196-03 Linden Blvd. St. Albans, NY 11412

"Changing Lives One Page At A Time."